Bar Talk:
A Comedy

RICHARD FOREMAN

First published by Sharpe Books in 2021.

CONTENTS

Introduction   i

Act One   1

Act Two   23

INTRODUCTION

Bar Talk can of course be read as a script, but a play should ideally be performed too. Should you read this book and be interested in hosting a production (whether you are an actor, director, drama teacher or even someone who owns a bar) then do please get in touch at richard@sharpebooks.com

The play is short - and the cast is small - partly because I wanted to write a script that could be staged easily. The play is also meant to have a drinks interval. One should not be wholly serious - or sober - when reading *Bar Talk* or seeing it performed.

Although it may not always feel like it, particularly at the end, *Bar Talk* is meant to be a comedy - albeit the humour may sometimes seem so black that it's difficult to see. I wanted to write something that would prove a tonic to the pandemic. I also wanted to write the piece as a pick me up for those people getting a headache over the rise of (for want of a better term) "wokery" - and a certain over-earnestness infecting society. Sarcasm is not the worst response or antidote to over-sincerity. It's healthy to laugh at the world and ourselves - especially with a drink in one's hand, in good company.

In short, enjoy the show.

Richard Foreman

Bar Talk.

Act One.

Robert, Charlotte and Rupert are in a bar. Enter Narrator.

Narrator: Evening. Imagine a bar in London, not wholly unlike this one. But nicer and friendlier. Only joking. It's a slow night, as slow as Chris Grayling or Diane Abbott. Patrons are trying to find answers at the bottom of a whisky glass. It's a good a place to look as any. Sitting over there is a regular, Robert Gatsby, an advertising copywriter. Robert may not have turned thirty, but he has seen enough of the world to not particularly want to see any more of it. Robert is a widower. His wife, Victoria, passed away a year ago. The spectre of his grief is still the most substantial thing in his life. You will notice how he still wears his wedding band and often twists the ring, when he thinks about Victoria. He has, unwittingly or otherwise, made his life smaller. He has few interests, and fewer friends. The world-weary soul keeps a bottle of sleeping pills in his bathroom cabinet. Or sometimes Robert keeps them in his pocket and pulls the bottle out, to stare at them, as though they were a little piece of heaven. His deliverance. On more than one occasion he has thought about taking an un-proscribed dose - and not waking up in the morning to the dream, or nightmare, of life. Yet, when drinking, as you will see, Robert can be good-humoured and good-natured. In his eyes, life is a comedy - which is, of course, its own tragedy. And this here is Charlotte. Charlotte is an actress, who is also a waitress. Although some might deem her a waitress, who also acts. She has been described as a budding actress, a promising actress and a talented actress. She would prefer to be a working actress. The soles of her shoes have become as worn out as a politician's word, trudging from audition to audition. Remarkably, Charlotte would still consider herself a glass half-full girl, despite often encountering the dregs. But false hope is still hope, I suppose. And, in terms of the hopeless, this is Rupert. Rupert is a self-proclaimed "social justice warrior," whatever that is, from Woking. His father would only agree to buy the neo-Marxist a flat in Camberwell if his son took on a part-time job. Rupert initially protested and defiantly argued that he would make his own way in life, but then he saw the prices of rental accommodation in the capital. Rupert would dearly like to cancel at least one in three of you in this audience. He will consider most of you as part of the problem, not the solution. He will feel intensely offended on your behalf, about an array of issues, for the remaining two thirds. If taking offence was an Olympic sport, he would win the silver medal – and feel grossly insulted that he did not win gold. Rupert, since studying Politics and Ecology at Goldsmiths University, has become incredibly serious-minded, which is, of course, its own comedy. I know that he has some preferred pronouns, but he keeps changing them and I can't quite keep up. Rupert recently wrote a blog piece, or his "manifesto" as he titled it, recounting his vision on how we can save the world. It involves a mixture of green taxes, giving youth a voice, and a five-year economic plan which would make Stalin blush. He also mentioned something about wind power. But it all seemed like hot air to me. If only God, which the student considers a cultural and patriarchal construct, could bestow upon him the powers to change the planet - and all of you - for the better. All I can say, with some certainty, is that this play will not change the world - or any of you - for the better.

Exit Narrator.

Charlotte: Hi Robert, same again?

Robert: Aye. I've been accused of drinking too much. But I would argue I drink just the right amount, or not quite enough.

Charlotte: How are you this evening?

Robert: If only my spirits were as high as my cholesterol levels. I may have to make it a long night, as it's been a long day. Too many meetings. I've seen, or suffered, too many people.

Charlotte: You don't much like people, do you?

Robert: No. Nor would you much like people, Charlotte, if you knew them as well as I do. We men are wretched creatures, to quote Homer. Man is born to trouble, as the sparks fly upwards, to quote Job.

Charlotte: And what about women?

Robert: Woman, that was God's second mistake, to quote Nietzsche. But women are really much nicer than men. No wonder we like them. Kingsley Amis. I am quoting other people because I have nothing to say for myself, unfortunately. If only other people realised that they have nothing to say for themselves, instead of incessantly yammering on - which I am aware I may be doing now - then I might have made it here for happy hour earlier. I do not like to suffer fools gladly, but I am all too glad when fools suffer.

Charlotte: You should not joke about such things.

Robert: I wasn't aware that I was joking. At best I am only ever half-joking. If you think that I'm joking, I'm probably being serious, Charlotte. If you think that I am being serious, I'm doubtless joking.

Charlotte: Well, I take it that you weren't joking when you asked for another drink. I'll get it for you.

Charlotte goes across to Rupert to fix Robert a drink.

Rupert: Hmm, I see that *he's* in again.

Charlotte: Do you mean Robert?

Rupert: Yes. You do know that he works in advertising?

Charlotte: I know. So what?

Rupert: So what?! Advertising is basically industrialised deception. Advertising propagates a false consciousness. All big advertisers are big polluters. Advertising is a lubricant for capitalism. And I have warned you about the evils of capitalism before.

Charlotte: Yes. Once or twice.

Rupert: It's like he lies for a living.

Charlotte: I would like to act for a living. You say that you would like to write for a living. There's more that unites us than divides us. You seem a bit flustered and het up for another reason, though. Is everything okay?

Rupert: I know. I shouldn't snap at you, for his crimes. Also, a customer over there has just referred to me, using the wrong pronoun, again. He even overheard me mention the correct pronouns to use when I was talking to another customer. I want to be referred to as ze, or perself. It's my truth. When I corrected him, he said that I was being ridiculous. Me? Ridiculous? I have a degree from Goldsmith University and a successful blog. What does he have? I feel like finding out where he works and writing an email to his boss. Or I should out him on Twitter. Cancel him. People can be so intolerant.

Charlotte: Yes, they can – and sometimes without even knowing it.

Charlotte walks over to Robert, to serve him his drink.

Robert: Thank you. So, how's the acting going?

Charlotte: It's going to hell, it seems. I'm still playing the part of the plucky waitress, I'm afraid.

Robert: When you're going through hell, keep going. Winston Churchill.

Charlotte: I actually have an audition tomorrow morning, to play Ophelia. I'm not sure if I am going to attend, though. I only got the call today. I haven't had the time to learn the scene properly. I get off my shift soon, but I feel like I'll probably just fall asleep when I get home.

Robert: Can I help? Believe it or not but I played the part of Hamlet, many moons ago, when I was in college. I can run through your lines with you if you like. I can't promise that I won't bore you to sleep before you reach home, however.

Charlotte: Really?! I don't want to put you to any trouble.

Robert: There are worse ways to spend an evening, than reciting or listening to Shakespeare. How weary, stale, flat, and unprofitable seem to me all the uses of this world!

Charlotte: I just need to clock off. This drink - and the next one - are on me, as a thank you.

Robert: That's very kind. Perhaps the world isn't so weary, stale, flat, and unprofitable after all.

Charlotte walks over to Rupert and collects her bag. She retrieves a copy of Hamlet.

Rupert: You look like the cat who has got the cream, not that one should give cats dairy products. When I owned a cat, I only gave it vegan food. Unfortunately, it died. The capitalist didn't actually give you a tip, did he? It would be a rare instance of him re-distributing his wealth.

Charlotte: No. Robert said he would help me read through my lines for an audition tomorrow. I'm not sure whether I'm more nervous or excited. I could do with a large vodka, to help wash away the butterflies in my stomach.

Rupert: Oh. Well, I would have helped you with your lines if you would have only asked.

Charlotte: Sorry, I didn't know. Do you read Shakespeare?

Rupert: No, I read Owen Jones and Manga.

Charlotte: Not to worry.

Rupert: But I do worry about you.

Charlotte: What was that?

Rupert: Oh, nothing.

Charlotte returns to Robert's table, holding open a copy of Hamlet.

Charlotte: Are you sure that you want to do this?

Robert: Nothing is good or bad but thinking makes it so. You're not feeling any stage fright, I hope.

Charlotte: No. Strangely, I feel fine. Did you garner any reviews for your performance, years ago?

Robert: Unfortunately, or fortunately, not. The editor of the college newspaper was a former girlfriend. She got to know me well enough to not particularly like me.

Charlotte: The audition will cover part of Act III. Are you sure that you will be able to remember the lines?

Robert: Yes, I should be fine. I sometimes wish that my memory was not so sharp, when I remember Victoria.

Charlotte: Sorry, what did you say?

Robert: Oh, nothing.

Charlotte: Well, here goes nothing…
Good my lord.
How does your honour for this many a day?

Robert: I humbly thank you: well, well, well.

Charlotte: My lord, I have remembrances of yours
That I have longed to redeliver.
I pray you, now receive them.

Robert: No, not I!
I never gave you aught.

Charlotte: My honour'd lord, you know right well
you did,
And with them words of so sweet breath compos'd
As made the things more rich. Their perfume lost,
Take these gifts; for to the noble mind
Rich gifts wax poor when givers prove unkind.

There, my lord.

Robert: Ha, ha! Are you honest?

Charlotte: My lord?

Robert: Are you fair?

Charlotte: What means your lordship?

Robert: That if you be honest and fair, your honesty should admit no discourse to your beauty.

Charlotte: Could beauty, my lord, have better commerce than with honesty?

Robert: Ay, truly; for the power of beauty will sooner transform honesty from what it is to a bawd than the force of honesty can translate beauty into its likeness. This was sometime a paradox, but now the time gives it proof. I did love you once.

Charlotte: Indeed, my lord, you made me believe so.

Robert: You should not have believed me; for virtue cannot so inoculate our old stock but we shall relish of it. I loved you not.

Charlotte: I was the more deceived.

Robert: Get thee to a nunnery! Why wouldst thou be a breeder of sinners? I am myself indifferent honest, but yet I could accuse me of such things that it were better my mother had not borne me. I am very proud, revengeful, ambitious; with more offences at my beck than I have thoughts to put them in, imagination to give them shape, or time to act them in. What should such fellows as I do, crawling between earth and heaven? We are arrant knaves all; believe none of us. Go thy ways to a nunnery. Where's your father?

Charlotte: At home, my lord.

Robert: Let the doors be shut upon him, that he may play the fool nowhere but in his own house. Farewell.

Charlotte: O, help him, you sweet heavens!

Robert: If thou dost marry, I'll give thee this plague for thy dowry: be thou as chaste as ice, as pure as snow, thou shalt not escape calumny. Get thee to a nunnery. Go, farewell. Or if thou wilt needs marry, marry a fool; for wise men know well enough what monsters you make of them. To a nunnery, go; and quickly too. Farewell.

Charlotte: O heavenly powers, restore him!

Robert: I have heard of your paintings too, well enough. God hath given you one face, and you make yourselves another. You jig, you amble, and you lisp; and nickname God's creatures and make your wantonness your ignorance. Go to, I'll no more on't!

It hath made me mad. I say, we will have no more marriages. Those that are married - all but one - shall live; the rest shall keep as they are. To a nunnery, go.

Charlotte: O, what a noble mind is here o'erthrown!

The courtier's, scholar's, soldier's, eye, tongue, sword,

The expectancy and rose of the fair state,

The glass of fashion and the mould of form,

The observed of all observers, quite, quite down!

And I, of ladies most dejected and wretched,

That suck'd the honey of his music vows,

Now see that noble and most sovereign reason,

Like sweet bells jangled, out of tune and harsh;

That unmatch'd form and feature of blown youth

Blasted with ecstasy. O, woe is me,

To have seen what I have seen, see what I see!

Narrator: And scene. And at that moment Charlotte realised how much she liked Robert. Or even loved him. For Robert, it was too soon to fall in love again. But for Charlotte, love could not come too soon enough. She was used to men putting her on a pedestal, but mainly to look up her skirt. She had mainly dated actors - and the cast will attest that there are Kardashians less self-absorbed than thespians. Actors are the very soul of narcissism, whilst being unable to spell the word. But this feeling Charlotte now experienced was different, finer. Robert was different. Better. The regular had never hit on her, unlike scores of other customers. Customers. The C-word. But she now wanted to hit on him, to show him how attractive she thought he was. To show him that she cared. He was Hamlet. He needed saving. And she was Ophelia, willing to save him. If Robert did not quite feel the same as her then she would not falter. Charlotte had enough love, admiration and affection for the both of them, she considered. Unrequited love is still love - or at least the silhouette of love. And love can nourish and satisfy, even more than chocolate and alcohol. Yet, if Robert felt somehow nourished and satisfied, it was due to being able to help-out the young waitress, so she could become a young actress. Although he now stared at Charlotte, Robert was picturing Victoria - and how she would gaze at him fondly whenever he would recite a poem, by Byron or Tennyson, or quote Shakespeare, out of the blue.

Exit Narrator.

Charlotte: Wow. I don't quite know what to say.

Robert: The rest is silence, it seems, so to speak. But you were great. Very convincing.

Charlotte: Do you really think so?

Robert: Well, we are arrant knaves, all. Believe none of us. I also work in advertising, so shouldn't be trusted.

Charlotte: What does you work entail - if you do not mind me asking?

Robert: I spend the day making up trite slogans and bad puns. I'm a punny guy. My job is to basically convince you to buy something that you do not want or need, so I can then afford to buy things I do not want or need, along with non-house wine. There are worse fates I suppose. I just cannot think of them right now.

Charlotte: Being an out of work actress is not an enviable fate, either. I am all too familiar with the daytime TV schedule. I spend the day waiting for a call from my agent. When the phone does ring it is usually my mother, subtly or otherwise asking about if I am dating anyone. Everyone I seem to date is an arrant knave, at best, though. Every now and then, during the day, I even stand in front of the mirror and practise my reactions, imagining I have won an Oscar or Tony award.

Robert: Be careful about looking at in the mirror too much, lest you lose sight of yourself. But all will be well, Charlotte. You will get the part. If you don't,

I will still leave a bottle of non-house champagne for you here on ice. There is also someone out there for you, worth dating.

Charlotte: I know. Let me take your number. I will message you if I get the part. It will be nice to drink to celebrate, rather than commiserate, for once.

Enter Narrator.

Narrator: When Charlotte sent Robert a quick message, to confirm that she had his number, her thumb hovered over the phone as she tried to decide whether to end the text with an X - a kiss. She did not want to come across as too forward, but a kiss could convey the thousand words that were stuck in her throat. That night, after getting home, Charlotte kept her phone to hand, hoping that Robert would get in touch. To send her a message - and end it with an X. She could not stop thinking about him, thoughts as moreish as chocolate and alcohol put together. The widower was marriage material. Meanwhile, when Robert reached home, he could not stop thinking about Victoria - again. His heart ached so much so he wanted to cut it out. He missed hearing her laugh. Making her laugh. He missed her smell so much that, occasionally, he would spray her perfume in the bedroom. He vomited and wept, as he continued to drink. The bottle of Talisker was soon less than half empty. Whisky is the medicine of despair, to quote Graham Greene. Robert did not quite vomit and weep as much as when the hospital called that fateful night, informing him that his wife had been in a serious car accident. Part of him wanted to perish that evening. To be with his wife, for better or worse. Part of him wanted to die now, as he clasped the bottle of sleeping pills in his pocket and thought how Hamlet had only found some peace in the final act. But Robert was either too brave or too cowardly to unscrew the bottle. And scene.

Act Two.

Narrator: The audition went well. Charlotte remembered to take a breath before going on stage - a valuable tip from Robert. The Hamlet she acted with was a pretty boy - and a pretty dull boy - but she imagined that she was performing with Robert. For Robert. And soon after she received a call to say that she had got the part. Her heart was fit to bursting. Her glass over half full. Before contacting her agent or her mum, Charlotte called Robert. She wanted to hear his voice. See him. Thank him. Kiss him. Robert replied that he was due to go into a meeting, but he was pleased - and would keep his promise to buy the young actress a bottle of champagne to help celebrate. Charlotte arranged to swap her shift with Rupert, explaining that she wanted to go out and toast getting the part. Rupert was happy for his friend. He was less happy, however, when he found out that Charlotte was celebrating at the bar with the advertising copyrighter. The Tory. He cringed and winced as he said the word to himself, before scowling. The student, who was sweet on the actress, wanted to cancel Robert in more ways than one. He cursed the regular, using not the most pleasant pronouns in the world. To add insult to injury, Rupert was down in the rota to look after the section that they were sitting in. He asked a colleague to swap, but the colleague remembered how the week before Rupert had said that he had been brainwashed by the mainstream media and was a slave to the patriarchy. Rupert tried to stand as far away from the pair as possible, but to no avail. Every time Robert made Charlotte laugh it made the Marxist's teeth itch and his heart sink. At one point Rupert thought about using one of his troll accounts to abuse the capitalist cog on Twitter, but he remembered that the regular wasn't on Twitter. Rupert recalled that it was one of the reasons why Charlotte had said that she liked the older man. One of many.

Charlotte: I am not sure that I would have ever attended the audition, let alone secured the part, without you. And that's not just the drink talking. So, thank you.

Robert: You should have more confidence in yourself, Charlotte. You have a lot to offer the world. You're pretty, without being vain. You're intelligent, without being conceited. You have a sense of decency, a sense of humour and, when they don't make you wear the God-awful uniform, a sense of style.

Charlotte: You should be my agent. You're like no one I have ever met, Robert.

Robert: Is that a good thing?

Charlotte: Yes, trust me. Most men now look into their phones, if they are not looking in the mirror, when they talk to women nowadays. They think that the Ring Cycle was written by J. R. R. Tolkien and

Botticelli a pasta dish. You don't even need to be a snob to look down on the quality of men out there. Most of the men I have dated have more product in their hair than I do. You can quote Shakespeare. Usually, when I go out, I have someone quote how much a gram of cocaine costs. You're courteous, modest and witty. Your late wife was a lucky woman to have you.

Robert: I was the lucky one, trust me. If I'm courteous, it's because being rude is too exhausting. If I'm modest, it's because I have a lot to be modest about. And my sense of humour is no laughing matter.

Charlotte: You're funny, Robert. And funny is the new sexy.

Robert: Really? I wish it was the old sexy. My ex-girlfriend may then have granted me that review in the college newspaper. I dare say I can take the sexy out of funny, if needed. I can probably even take the sexy out of sexy, given a chance. But please excuse me, Charlotte, whilst I use the bathroom.

Charlotte: I will order us up another bottle. It's on me, no arguments. I will have to get the house champagne rather than Bollinger.

Robert: That's fine. Second best is good enough.

Robert leaves to go to the bathroom. Charlotte beckons Rupert to come over.

Charlotte: Can I order a bottle of the house champagne, please?

Rupert: Don't you think that you might have had enough? I don't want him trying to take advantage of you.

Charlotte: Well, I do. And he'll succeed. You seem to be in a mood tonight, Rupert. Has someone upset you again?

Rupert: Yes.

Charlotte: Who?

Rupert: No one. It's nothing. You seem to be in a strange mood too. I have never seen you like this before.

Charlotte: What, happy? You should try it too. You shouldn't take everything in life so seriously.

Rupert: Are you now saying that I should treat climate change, my mental health issues, my pronouns and critical race theory as a joke?

Charlotte: There are worse fates. I would just like to see you enjoy yourself more, Rupert. Smile more. Laugh more. You should try and find someone special.

Rupert: I thought I did.

Charlotte: Who?

Rupert: No one. I will get you your drinks.

Rupert leaves to arrange more drinks. Robert sits back down at the table.

Robert: So, when can I come see you in the production? Obviously, I just want to find out whether my Hamlet stands up to that of you co-star's performance.

Charlotte: The first show won't be for some time. I will let you know and arrange a ticket for you. But you can see me anytime. Just call me. I would like to see you again, if you're not seeing anyone at the moment.

Robert: You're sweet, Charlotte. So sweet that I worry you may be a danger to diabetics. But I think it's best that we don't see each other in that way.

Charlotte: Why? We're both free and available.

Robert: This may sound absurd, but I consider myself still married, even if I am married to a ghost. I am still in love with my late wife, Victoria. I feel like I would be being unfaithful if I started seeing you in earnest. I can't give anything of myself. I'm not sure if I have got anything left to give. I somehow think that it will be akin to a mortal sin if I ever marry again. Damn that Catholic school, brainwashing me as a child. It may be the case that a person only gets to fall in love once, at best, in this life. If they fall in love a second time, then the first may be just a pratfall. Don't get me wrong. I am no monk, Charlotte. I have been out with a few women since Victoria passed. But it was about sex, not love. I am human, all too human, after all. I know that I can be accused of being conceited or living in the past. I should move on, people tell me. I am aware that I may be wasting my life. But we all waste our lives in one way or another. Life is a joke - and the punchline is death.

Charlotte: You must love her very much.

Robert: Maybe too much. But Victoria was the best part of my day, which may not be that great a claim seeing as the rest of my time was spent in the company of witless advertising executives. Victoria was the soul of kindness - and sarcasm. She was a wonderful wife - and would have made a wonderful mother. I still miss her, every day. I still stupidly go to make her a cup of coffee in the morning for her. I still play her favourite songs, just in case she is in the room. I would give my life to see her again, just one more time. I am sorry if I have somehow led you on. You're one of the last people I would wish to hurt, unwittingly or otherwise, Charlotte. I can of course still be on call to get drunk with.

Charlotte: You have nothing to be sorry for. I just thought that... No, it's nothing. I just wish... No. I was the more deceived, it appears. You did not do anything wrong. It's just that everything seems wrong sometimes. My old drama teacher was right. The only true love stories are tragic love stories.

Robert: Aye. Unfortunately, life isn't like a play with a happy ending.

Charlotte: It would be nice if sometimes it was. Please, excuse me.

Robert: Are you okay? Have you got something in your eye?

Charlotte: No. It's nothing.

Charlotte exits. Rupert enters.

Rupert: Right, I have something that I need to say to you.

Pause.

Robert: Go on.

Rupert: You shouldn't be seeing Charlotte. She's too good for the likes of you.

Robert: I dare say that you are probably right.

Rupert: What?

Robert: I'm agreeing with you.

Rupert: Are you being sarcastic?

Robert: For once, I may be being sincere. Although I could of course be being sarcastic when I say that.

Rupert: You're too old for her.

Robert: You may be right.

Rupert: She deserves better than you.

Robert: Again, I am not going to disagree with you.

Rupert: Really? I am just not used to people agreeing with me - unless they're online.

Robert: It's Rupert, isn't it?

Rupert: Yes.

Robert: Please, take a seat for a moment Rupert. You look like you have the weight of the world on your shoulders. It's exhausting, trying to keep up with such nervous energy. You will be relieved to hear that I have just told Charlotte that I am not interested in pursuing any relationship with her.

Rupert: Why? What do you think is wrong with her? There must be something wrong with you.

Robert: There's plenty wrong with me, Rupert. But let us put that aside for now. I take it that you have the good sense and taste to like Charlotte?

Rupert: Yes.

Robert: Have you asked her out?

Rupert: No.

Robert: Why not, if you do not mind me asking?

Rupert: I've been busy. I write a blog.

Robert: A blog? Are you now being sarcastic? If you are putting more time and energy into a blog than you are Charlotte, then I would suggest that you do not deserve her either.

Rupert: But my blog is important. Greta Thunberg, or her publicist, once even liked one of my posts. We could be dealing with the end of the world, in relation to climate change. We need to take these things seriously.

Robert: We are forever dealing with the end of the world, in one way or another. You need to take Charlotte out to the theatre or to dinner. The world might not then feel like it's going to end. Instead of going home and telling everyone about how your day is going, ask Charlotte about her day.

Rupert: Yes. Should I be writing all this down? What other advice can you give me?

Robert: Normally I would encourage people to be themselves, but I'm not sure that would work in your case, Rupert. Tell me, why do you like Charlotte so much?

Rupert: She never laughs at me. Rather, she makes me laugh. Or at least smile. Or half-smile. Charlotte shows me sides to herself which she doesn't show others. She makes me want to be a different, better, person. I think she likes me too.

Robert: Well, we're about to find out. She's coming back. I will make myself scarce. Just talk to her, but don't mention any blog for God's sake.

Rupert: I'll try not to. Thanks. You're not as bad as I thought you were.

Robert: Now, we may have to disagree there. I could be worse.

Rupert: How are you going to make yourself scarce?

Robert: Don't worry, I'll make something up. I work in advertising. I lie for a living.

Charlotte enters.

Charlotte: I need a drink.

Robert: Excuse me, Charlotte, but I need a cigarette. I remember when the bars used to be thick with smoke - as thick as Chris Grayling or Diane Abbott - but I now need to go outside.

Robert exits.

Charlotte: I didn't even know he smoked.

Rupert: So, how's your evening going?

Charlotte: Not great. I think he's worth waiting for though.

Rupert: Well, he shouldn't be too long just smoking one cigarette.

Charlotte: No, I didn't mean that. Robert said that he isn't ready for a relationship, that he is still in love with his late wife. It may seem funny, or tragic, but I like him even more for still being faithful to her.

Rupert: Perhaps he will never be ready to fully move on. So you should.

Charlotte: I have got to give him a chance. Give myself a chance. Do you think that it's foolish to love someone who doesn't feel the same way in return?

Rupert: What would I know?

Charlotte: I am sure that he likes me. He just doesn't quite realise it yet. Robert makes me laugh. He makes me want to be a better person. I envy you, in a way, Rupert. You're free to focus on what you love, your causes and your blog. Emotions are overrated. Double-edged swords.

Rupert: I am starting to agree with you. Even I have certain feelings for certain people, though.

Charlotte: Oh, who?

Rupert: No one. You're right, you should wait for him. Second best shouldn't be good enough. You deserve someone special, Charlotte.

Charlotte: You're special too, Rupert. You will find someone, if you haven't got your eye on somebody already. Someone who cares about the planet and who will know which pronoun to use, even before you do. You should invite your mystery woman to my first performance. I will arrange a couple of tickets for you.

Rupert: I think I might be busy that night.

Charlotte: But even I do not know the date yet.

Rupert: Oh, yes. Sorry.

Charlotte: Promise me that you will be there. It would mean a lot to me.

Rupert: I promise.

Charlotte: And will the girl you like be there too?

Rupert: I can guarantee it. But I better get back to work. These drinks won't serve themselves, unless capitalism and the military-industrial complex automate even more of the labour force.

Robert encounters Rupert as he exits.

Robert: How did it go?

Rupert: Not that well. She's interested in someone else.

Robert exits.

Robert: Rupert's a nice chap. There's more to him than meets the eye.

Charlotte: Really?

Robert: Well, perhaps not. He just needs to laugh at himself more. He might then learn to laugh at a few other things in life.

Charlotte: People can lack self-awareness. Now, where were we?

Robert: Drinking, I think. There are worse fates.

Charlotte: Do you have any plans for tomorrow evening?

Robert: The same plans I had for last night and tonight. I will be here, but hopefully a bit earlier - for even happier hours.

Tomorrow, and tomorrow, and tomorrow,

Creeps in this petty pace from day to day,

To the last syllable of recorded time;

And all our yesterdays have lighted fools

The way to dusty death. Out, out, brief candle!

Life's but a walking shadow, a poor player,

That struts and frets his hour upon the stage,

And then is heard no more. It is a tale

Told by an idiot, full of sound and fury,

Signifying nothing.

But ignore me, Charlotte. We should be celebrating rather than commiserating. I can deal with depressing myself, but I should not be bringing others down to my wretched level. Do you have any nice plans for tomorrow night?

Charlotte: I may be here, working. If not, I may join you for a drink, if that's okay?

Robert: Happy hour just got happier. But you may want to think about taking your friend, Rupert, out. You will help take his mind off the end of the world.

Charlotte: He may be busy tomorrow. I have encouraged Rupert to ask out his mystery woman.

Robert laughs.

What? Why are you laughing?

Robert: God, life is tragic. The soul of misery. We seem fated to want what we can never have. But of course, one's reach should exceed one's grasp, or what's a heaven for? Robert Browning. And still I seem to have nothing to say for myself. But it's late. It's not dark yet, but it's getting there - to quote Bob Dylan. I'm starting to realise how tired I am, Charlotte. But all will be well. I just need to catch up on some reading and sleep. To sleep, perchance to dream. You need to time to learn your lines. I promised myself that I would finish off the last chapters of Graham Greene's *The Heart of the Matter.* I also need to meet an old friend. It's been a long time since I've seen them. Too long.

Charlotte: Oh, who?

Robert: No one. Forget everything I've said. You'll be all the happier for it. Let me settle the bill, before I go.

Enter Narrator.

Narrator: End scene. I think it best that we leave it there. I did say that the play would not change the world - or you all - for the better. I like to think that we have made good on our promise. I will leave it for you to judge whether any of our characters' lives were changed for the better. It was just some bar talk, after all. Thank you for watching.

Printed in Great Britain
by Amazon